STATHEAD SPORTS

STATHEAD
BASKETBALL
How Data Changed the Sport

by Michael Bradley

COMPASS POINT BOOKS
a capstone imprint

Stathead Sports is published
by Compass Point Books, a Capstone imprint
1710 Roe Crest Drive, North Mankato, Minnesota 56003
www.mycapstone.com

Library of Congress Cataloging-in-Publication Data is available on the Library
of Congress website.
ISBN 978-1-5435-1447-6 (library binding)
ISBN 978-1-5435-1451-3 (paperback)
ISBN 978-1-5435-1455-1 (eBook PDF)

Editorial Credits
Nick Healy, editor; Terri Poburka, designer; Eric Gohl, media researcher;
Laura Manthe, production specialist

AP Photo: Mark Duncan, 14, Rusty Kennedy, 20; Dreamstime: Jerry Coli, 8,
16; Newscom: EFE/George Frey, 40, EFE/Mike Brown, 37, 42, KRT/Philadelphia
Inquirer, 13, TNS/Aaron Lavinsky, 45, TNS/David Santiago, 26, TNS/Ray Chavez,
34, USA Today Sports/Bob Donnan, 24, USA Today Sports/Geoff Burke, cover,
USA Today Sports/Jerome Miron, 31, USA Today Sports/John E. Sokolowski, 28,
USA Today Sports/Kyle Terada, 6, 23, USA Today Sports/Nelson Chenault, 4, USA
Today Sports/Raj Mehta, 38; Shutterstock: cristovao, back cover, 19

Design Elements: Shutterstock

Printed in the United States of America.
PA017

TABLE OF CONTENTS

WINNING BIG WITH BETTER PASSING

▲ Under coach Steve Kerr, Stephen Curry and the Warriors began focusing on speedy, crisp ball movement to create more open shots.

Steve Kerr took over as head coach of the Golden State Warriors before the 2014–15 season. From the start, Kerr wanted to make changes. Big changes. The Warriors had won 51 games the year before. Not a bad result. But the team lost in the first round of the playoffs. They were good but not good enough.

Like many National Basketball Association (NBA) teams, the 2013–14 Warriors had used a lot of one-on-one play on offense. They were successful, but Kerr believed the team could do better. He wanted his players to pass more. A lot more. In fact, he wanted them to pass the ball 300 times a game. That wouldn't be easy. The previous season Golden State averaged just 243.8 passes per game, dead last in the NBA. Kerr thought that had to change.

The change took some time. But as the 2014–15 season went on, the Warriors shared the ball more. Then they shared it a lot more. By season's end, they had moved up to ninth in the NBA in passes per game, with an average of 306.6. The change helped the Warriors win 16 more games than a season earlier. They also won the franchise's first championship in 40 years. The Warriors had great talent on their roster, but they didn't win big until they focused on sharing the ball.

▶ Steve Kerr played on five NBA championship teams during his days as a sharp-shooting guard. The Warriors gave him his first job as a head coach.

The NBA has always been big on numbers. Points, assists, and rebounds have long been used to measure a player's performance. Those numbers provide the game's main individual stats. Players are also tracked for their shooting percentage, blocked shots, and steals. And teams have long been interested in how successfully they score, rebound, and defend.

Players and coaches never forget about the most basic NBA number—24. That's how many seconds a team has to shoot each time it possesses the ball.

Those are the basics. Today, NBA franchises are more interested in numbers than ever before. And they are willing to dig deeper into statistics to find ways to win. Back in 2014, Kerr and the Warriors decided that increased and improved passing was the key to success. Kerr's approach made sense. More ball movement puts the defense on the move and creates more open shots.

But there are other ways of breaking down the numbers. NBA teams want to know how efficient they are on both ends of the court. They are interested in how players compare to opponents in all parts of the game—not just in how many points they score. Coaches want to know how many passes are thrown during every game and, more importantly, whether those passes lead to baskets. And when it comes to shooting, they want to know who is best inside the three-point arc, outside the arc, and from anywhere on the court.

The NBA seems to get more exciting every season. And with advanced statistics, teams and fans can learn more about their favorite players and how they measure up.

SETTING HIGH STANDARDS

▶ Kareem Abdul-Jabbar (right) used his famous skyhook to rack up points on his way to the league's career scoring record.

CHAPTER 2

DON'T BE FOOLED

▶ Dan Issel (44) was part of a high-flying offense for the Denver Nuggets in the early 1980s.

that year stood out was that he shot 61.3 percent from the free throw line, his best performance ever in that category. (Wilt was known to be a poor foul shooter.) It's also amazing because he scored 100 points in a single game—on March 2, 1962, against the New York Knicks. That remains the record for points in a single game. The closest anybody has come to it was Kobe Bryant's 81 points against the Toronto Raptors in 2006. Also that season, Chamberlain pulled down a record 43 rebounds in a triple-overtime loss to the Lakers.

For years, points and rebounds have been the simplest statistics by which NBA players have been measured each game. Fans want to know who won, and then they want to know who led the way. For much of his career, Chamberlain did that. So did Jordan. Today, James Harden and Russell Westbrook are usually found at the top of the scoring list when they play. Stephen Curry and LeBron James also pile up the points. And so does the Bucks' Giannis Antetokounmpo. The Los Angeles Clippers' DeAndre Jordan can be counted on to score and to snag a bunch of rebounds.

When it comes to assists, John Stockton is the all-time king. The former Utah Jazz point guard holds the career record for most assists. He led the league in the category nine straight seasons.

In 2017–18, Westbrook averaged 10.3 assists per game to lead the league. He regularly notched triple-doubles,

meaning he reached double figures in points, rebounds, and assists. He averaged a triple-double for the season. That feat had been accomplished only twice before in NBA history. Oscar Robertson did it for the Cincinnati Royals in 1961–62, and Westbrook did it in 2016–17.

The NBA didn't start keeping track of steals as an official statistic until 1973–74. Perhaps it was only fitting that in the first year Larry Steele led the league. The Portland Trail Blazers guard averaged 2.68 steals per game. Stars such as Michael Jordan and Allen Iverson were well-known ball thieves. Both led the league three times. Point guard Chris Paul, now of the Houston Rockets, has topped the list six times. He did it in four straight seasons from 2010–14 while with the New Orleans Hornets and the Clippers.

Just as the NBA waited several years to recognize steals as a key stat, blocked shots were also ignored until 1973–74. That year Elmore "The Human Eraser" Smith led the league with 4.85 blocks per game, which is still the third-best average ever.

Standing 7-feet-4-inches tall, the Jazz's Mark Eaton holds the record with 5.56 blocks per game in 1984–85. In more recent seasons, Anthony Davis, Serge Ibaka, and Dwight Howard have each topped the list twice.

Team stats also play an important role in the NBA. Much can be learned about a team by tracking its averages for points scored and points allowed. Coaches

and followers of the game also pay attention to a team's field goal percentage and opposing field goal percentage. The first of these stats shows how efficient a team is on offense. The second shows how well they prevent rivals from scoring. (Usually a dogged defense will drive down the other team's shooting percentage.)

The numbers fans have studied for many seasons still matter, and it's important to understand them. But big numbers don't always help teams win.

WILT HITS 100

It's crazy to think about this today, but only 4,124 people watched Wilt Chamberlain score 100 points against the Knicks on March 2, 1962. Back then, the NBA played many games in smaller cities that didn't have their own teams. Chamberlain's big game was played in Hershey, a small town in central Pennsylvania.

Local fans who turned up at the arena saw quite a show. Wilt set a scoring record that will probably never be broken, in the Warriors' 169-147 victory. (The team moved from Philadelphia to San Francisco the next season.) Three defenders—Willie Naulls, Darrell Imhoff, and Cleveland Buckner—tried but failed to contain Chamberlain, who played every minute of the game.

Chamberlain started quickly, scoring 23 points in the first quarter. By halftime, he had 41. After three quarters, the total was 69, and people started wondering whether he could get to the century mark. In the final 12 minutes, Chamberlain shot 21 times, as his teammates fed him the ball every possession. Meanwhile, the Knicks surrounded him each time he touched the ball and fouled the other Warriors to prevent Chamberlain from getting possession. But he was unstoppable. He scored the 100th point on a layup with 46 seconds left. About 200 fans rushed onto the floor to celebrate.

▲ Wilt Chamberlain (right) and Celtics legend Bill Russell (left) battled in many games. Chamberlain's 100-point night came against lesser defenders.

Chamberlain made 36-of-63 field goal tries (57.1 percent) and was 28-of-32 (87.5 percent) from the foul line. That was remarkable, since he was a career 54 percent shooter from the line. It was just another memorable part of an amazing night.

It's not a good idea to declare that a feat in sports history will never be matched. Too many times players have broken records that once seemed completely out of reach. When Wilt Chamberlain retired in 1973, his career record of 31,419 points was considered untouchable. At the time the next closest person on the all-time points list was Lakers great Elgin Baylor, with 23,149. Chamberlain's mark looked safe.

It wasn't. Kareem Abdul-Jabbar had entered the NBA four seasons before Chamberlain left the game. By the time he was finished, Abdul-Jabbar surpassed Wilt's mark. In fact Abdul-Jabbar zoomed far ahead, scoring a total of 38,387 points.

Perhaps Chamberlain was unhappy to fall from the top of that list. But Wilt was able to enjoy the fact that his 1961–62 season numbers will never be beaten. That's right. We said it. Nobody is going to average 50.4 points per game (PPG) for an entire season ever again. Bet on it.

You know why? Consider who is second on the list. It's Wilt Chamberlain, with 44.8 PPG in 1962–63. He's third too, with 38.4 PPG in 1960–61. And fourth, with 37.6 PPG in 1959–60. The only person who has come close to matching Chamberlain is, well, Chamberlain. Michael Jordan ranks fifth with 37.1 PPG in 1986–87. That's more than 13 points off the big man's pace.

The 1961–62 season was remarkable for Chamberlain, who was in only his third year in the NBA. One reason

An NBA general manager once said that even if a team loses 115-87 somebody has to score the 87 points. In other words, it's possible to put up a high average as a scorer but never really help a team win. Basic stats like average points or rebounds per game are useful, but high averages don't always add up to wins.

It's important for fans to understand that simply putting up big numbers isn't a guarantee of success. Consider the 1981–82 Denver Nuggets. The team averaged 126.5 points per game (PPG), the most ever by an NBA team. The team won 46 games with 36 losses in the regular season. The Nuggets finished second in their division. But they got bounced in the first round of the playoffs. Why did they fail in the postseason? Perhaps because they played awful defense, giving up 126.0 PPG during the regular season. That was the worst in the league—by a long shot. The next team at the bottom of the list gave up almost 10 points fewer per regular-season game. In the playoff series loss to the Phoenix Suns, Denver surrendered 121 points per game.

One key to success in the NBA is being able to beat the top teams. Doing that requires players who can play well when the defense is tighter, the opposing offense is more effective, and things don't come so easily. With 82 games in a season, many talented players can rack up big numbers. The champions are those who can deliver top performances when the games mean the most.

▲ Michael Jordan led the Chicago Bulls to six titles.

Michael Jordan won 10 regular-season scoring titles during his career and averaged 30.1 PPG. In the playoffs, however, his average actually went up. He averaged 33.4 per postseason game. He also had higher averages in rebounds and assists.

CHAPTER 3

PEAK EFFICIENCY

▶ Magic Johnson (left) led the Lakers' fast-paced offense in the early 1980s.

On Nov. 22, 1950, the Fort Wayne Pistons defeated the Minneapolis Lakers, 19-18, in the lowest-scoring NBA game ever. At that time, pro games were often boring. Teams stalled and held the ball, and fans weren't coming out to watch.

Something had to be done.

In 1954, the NBA introduced the 24-second shot clock. Syracuse Nationals (now Philadelphia 76ers) owner Danny Biasone and general manager Leo Ferris are credited with the concept. Biasone thought that games in which teams took at least 60 shots each were the most entertaining. So, he divided the number of seconds in a 48-minute NBA game (2,880) by 120 (60 shots per team) and got 24. Ferris helped convince the NBA to adopt that number.

In 1953–54, the last season without a shot clock, NBA teams averaged 79 points per game. The next year, they averaged 93, and the number jumped to 107 by 1957–58. The fans noticed. Within a few years of the shot clock's introduction, attendance increased by 40 percent.

It isn't always the best way to measure a player's unselfishness. First off, there is no set definition of an assist. Some teams give a player credit for one if he passes to someone who takes two dribbles and then hits a three-pointer. That's not exactly a pass that leads directly to a basket. But some teams give players an assist for that pass to boost their statistics.

Steals, too, can be misleading. Some players pile them up by hanging out in the passing lanes, waiting to jump on lazy dishes. They look like great defenders, when in reality, they are trying to pile up numbers while not paying close attention to the players they are supposed to be guarding. Someone could get two steals a game, but his man scores 25 on him. That doesn't show up in the box score, but it certainly hurts his team's cause.

So, what is a fan to do? There are statistics out there that measure players' efficiency ratings and reveal how much they help their teams win. These stats are about more than how many points players score. These stats show what players do and how they prevent opponents from being successful. Read on and you'll see how advanced stats can prove who the NBA's best players and teams really are.

LeBron James also gets better when the games mean more. Through the 2016–17 season, he scored 27.2 PPG during regular season and 28.4 in postseason contests. In games against tougher and more motivated competition, Jordan and James were better than they were against the rest of the league.

That's impressive. Those numbers meant something in terms of helping their teams win.

As the Nuggets showed, scoring averages can be misleading, but so can other stats. Fans love to watch big-time shot blockers. They swat opponents' shots into the stands. Then they growl, wag fingers, and warn the other team to stay away from the basket. It's entertaining stuff. It's also not a very accurate way of showing whether a player is a good defender.

A player may be great at blocking shots, but he may slack off his own man to play flyswatter in the lane. A savvy opponent will prey on this and dump a pass to the open man. An easy basket may follow. How a player gets his blocks is as important as how many he gets. There is a lot more to good defense in the NBA than knocking the ball out of the air. Players have to position themselves well. They have to help their teammates. They have to fit into a team concept.

Speaking of helping out, a player's assist total seems like a perfect way to judge who's a good teammate. But fans should be a bit wary of this stat.

From 1977 to 2015 only one team ranked in the NBA's top five in pace—the number of possessions per 48 minutes—and won the league's championship. The 1981–82 Los Angeles Lakers ranked fifth and beat the Philadelphia 76ers in the Finals.

For many years, experts believed that teams playing too fast were easy targets in the postseason. In the playoffs teams tightened up on defense, and half-court basketball ruled. Most experts thought playoff basketball meant the jackrabbits wouldn't be able to run free. They wouldn't get shots off as easily and wouldn't survive at the defensive end against tougher teams. And for a long time, those experts were right.

Along came Stephen Curry and the Warriors, and everything changed. Golden State finished second in the NBA in pace in 2014–15 with 101.0 possessions per 48 minutes. And they won the championship. The next year they were second again (103.0) and raced back to the Finals. The Cleveland Cavaliers toppled the Warriors that time around, but in 2016–17, Golden State was running again. The Warriors slipped to third in possessions per regulation game but slightly upped their pace to 103.6. They reclaimed the big trophy in the Finals.

With the success of the Warriors, the pace-and-space approach didn't look like such a bad idea. More teams looked to spread the floor and increase scoring opportunities. In fact, teams all over the NBA decided to speed things up. In 2014–15, only six teams averaged 100 or more possessions per 48 minutes. In 2015–16, that number swelled to 13, and the next season it was 16. It looked like the whole league was using jet fuel.

That's why *pace* is a popular word in today's NBA. Teams pay close attention to their pace and total possessions. The more possessions, the more likely a team is to score a lot of points. That's unless the team can't make any shots, of course. As a statistic, pace also shows the number of times an opponent has the ball. And if the other guys have it a lot, they also have the chance to score often.

A high number in pace is no guarantee of success. In the 2016–17 season, eight of the 16 teams that topped 100 possessions per game didn't reach the playoffs. But the Golden State model remains popular. Those rebuilding teams are trying to copy the Warriors while adding players who can succeed in a fast-paced plan.

The Warriors' coaches and players focus on pace. The team plays fast. They run the court and move the ball quickly. With players like Kevin Durant, Steph Curry, Klay Thompson, and Draymond Green, the more times they have the ball, the better. In the 2017 Finals, the Warriors and Cavs played at a brisk tempo, and Golden State coach Steve Kerr was quite happy with that.

"They're at their best when they're playing fast. We are too," Kerr said after the second game of the series.

▶ Klay Thompson can pass and shoot with the league's best.

"We like the pace, they like the pace. It makes for better team basketball. It comes down to who executes, who takes care of the ball, who gets back in transition. It's a fun style."

While pushing the pace, teams also want to be efficient. It doesn't matter how many times a team has the ball if it can't score—and keep the other team from doing so. Teams measure their efficiency by looking at how many points they score per 100 possessions. This stat is calculated by taking the number of points a team scores, dividing by total possessions, and multiplying that number by 100.

Which team had the highest offensive efficiency in 2016–17? You guessed it: Golden State. The Warriors scored 113.2 points per 100 possessions. The Cavs, who lost to the Warriors in the Finals, were third with 110.9 points per 100 possessions.

Calculating defensive efficiency is more difficult. That number is found by a complicated formula. It starts with subtracting the opponents' offensive rebounds from their field goals attempted. Then turnovers are added. Total free throws are multiplied by 0.4 and added to the previous sum. All of that math will yield the number of opposing possessions. Then you divide points scored by possessions and multiply by 100.

Want to know why the Warriors won the NBA title in 2017? They were the most efficient offensive team and the second-most efficient defensive team, behind the Spurs. The Warriors gave up 101.1 points per 100 possessions.

In other words, per 100 possessions, the Warriors were 12.1 points per game better than their opponents.

That's pretty darn good.

Judging by Golden State's postseason success, no wonder other teams are pushing the pace too.

▲ Steph Curry and LeBron James clashed in the Finals three seasons in a row.

REGULAR SEASON RECORD

Even though the 2015–16 Warriors lost the NBA Finals to Cleveland, it's easy to make the argument that Golden State was the best regular-season team in NBA history.

First off, the Warriors won 73 games, one more than Chicago did in 1995–96, to set the previous NBA record. Perhaps the most impressive thing about that was that coach Steve Kerr missed the first 43 games of the season while recovering from back surgery. Assistant Luke Walton led the Warriors to a 39-4 record to start the year.

Golden State led the league in team field goal percentage (48.7), three-point percentage (41.6), and two-point percentage (52.8). The Warriors scored more points per game (114.9) and had more assists per game (28.9) than any other team. They had the most efficient offense (114.5 points per 100 possessions) in the league and the top effective field goal percentage (56.3) and the second-best defensive effective field goal percentage (47.9). Golden State was second in blocks per game (6.1) and in opposing three-point field goal percentage (33.2).

The season may not have ended the way fans wanted, but the Warriors were outstanding for 82 games—and perhaps the best ever during that stretch.

CHAPTER 4

INDIVIDUAL EFFORT

▶ Chris Paul helped the Rockets improve in 2017–18.

When the Rockets traded for Chris Paul during the summer of 2017, some fans worried. Would another guard who liked to have the ball in his hands slow down James Harden? Would Harden's numbers and effectiveness overall decline? Since joining the Rockets, Harden had been one of the league's most dynamic players. But he couldn't be dynamic without the ball. Adding Paul sounded good to some people, but others thought it had potential to be a big problem.

Halfway through the 2017–18 season, those fears were gone. Paul didn't hurt Harden's game. The Beard, as Harden is known, seemed to be even better than before. He led the league in just about every major overall advanced statistical category. He was at or close to the top in real plus-minus, win shares, player efficiency rating, and usage rate. While people were talking about whether LeBron James was having his best year ever, Harden was making a good case for the MVP award.

"[In 2016–17] I thought he was unbelievable," Houston coach Mike D'Antoni said. "Now I guess I've got to come up with a new word. I don't know what he is this year. He's gone up another level, which I didn't think was possible."

▼ James Harden (right) led the Rockets to the NBA's best record in 2017–18.

For many, the fact that Harden led the league in scoring in 2017–18 was enough. But the other numbers demonstrated just how big an impact he was having on the court. For instance, his usage rate number (36.1 percent) showed just how important he was to the Rockets' offense. Usage rate measures how involved a player is when his team has the ball. On 36.1 percent of Houston's plays during the season, Harden either shot the ball, got to the free throw line, or turned it over. Harden was one of five Rockets on the floor at any moment, of course. And he didn't play every minute of every game. Still, he played the key role in more than one-third of his team's plays.

Clearly, the 2017–18 Rockets relied on Harden. A lot. But what did he do with the ball when he had it so much? The answer is simple: plenty. And the numbers show it.

Real plus-minus measures how well a team does when a certain player is on the floor. For many years, teams used normal plus-minus calculations to figure that out. They looked at how many points the team scored when the player was on the court, versus how many the other team put up. Pretty simple, right? But its usefulness was limited. It had obvious flaws. A player's normal plus-minus didn't consider the skill of the opposing team or of the other players on his own team.

Real plus-minus (RPM) is far more complicated, but

it aims to reflect the quality of the other people on the court. RPM looks at every NBA possession in a season (about 230,000) and calculates how many points a player adds or subtracts, on average, to his team's net scoring per 100 possessions played. The stat allows us to compare each player with his teammates to determine how much of an impact he has on his team's success. When Harden finished second in the NBA with a 6.41 RPM, it meant the Rockets were 6.41 points better than their opponents when Harden was on the court.

The 2017–18 season was only the fifth year that the real plus-minus stat had been used in the NBA. That might have made it hard to figure out how impressive Harden was. One way to do it is to look at LeBron James, who has finished first in RPM for three of the previous four seasons. He was second to Steph Curry in the other. His best RPM was 9.79, in 2015–16. He's not King James for nothing.

While RPM is tough to calculate, player efficiency rating (PER) may be even more difficult. PER takes into account every positive thing a player does on the court. That includes points, rebounds, assists, steals, blocks, and more. And PER subtracts the bad things—turnovers, missed shots, etc. It then applies them to minutes played and the number of possessions a player takes part in. Every season, the NBA average is set at 15. In 2017–18, Harden's PER was 29.87, or nearly twice the average.

In 2016–17, Oklahoma City's Russell Westbrook had the best PER. In 2015–16 it was Curry. The 2014–15 leader was Pelicans center Anthony Davis, and in 2013–14, Kevin Durant led the way.

The bottom line in the NBA is total wins, and Harden had a big impact on that in 2017–18. The Rockets were 65–17, and Harden had a league-leading win share of 15.4. That meant he was directly responsible for 15.4 (or 24 percent) of the team's wins. In 2016–17, he had a league-best win share of 15.0, or 27.3 percent, of the Rockets' 55 triumphs. It was impressive, but not as good as his dominance in 2017–18.

RPM and PER are good tools for showing how effective players are. But in recent seasons the NBA has become even more sophisticated in how it measures performance. Beginning in 2010 four NBA teams began using SportVU

▼ LeBron James has shined for years, and his RPM numbers show his impact on the court.

technology to track the movements of every player during every possession of every game. By 2013 every NBA arena had six SportVU cameras to track the action.

SportVU cameras observe real-time player movement 25 times per second. They register every touch, pass, dribble, shot, rebound, or other basketball movement. And they feed teams advanced statistics that help them decide what works and what doesn't.

SportVU can help coaches make better decisions before and during games. It can even show when a player's performance is dropping—possibly due to overwork or injury. That way, coaches can limit a player's minutes during crucial times of the season and keep him from getting hurt.

The result is a more in-depth look at the game for coaches and fans. The NBA made SportVU's stats available to all in 2016. All of this data allows a greater ability to understand why teams win or lose.

PER LEADERS

Player efficiency rating (PER) takes into account every positive thing a player does on the court (points, rebounds, assists, steals, blocks, etc.) and subtracts the bad things (turnovers, missed shots, etc). It takes the number and applies it to the number of minutes played and the number of possessions a player takes part in. The NBA average is set at 15.

Career PER Leaders

PLAYER	TEAM(S)	PER
Michael Jordan	Bulls/Wizards	27.9
LeBron James	Heat/Cavaliers	27.7
Shaquille O'Neal	Magic/Lakers/Heat/Suns/Cavaliers/Celtics	26.4
David Robinson	Spurs	26.2
Wilt Chamberlain	Warriors/76ers/Lakers	26.1

2016–17 PER Leaders

PLAYER	TEAM(S)	PER
Russell Westbrook	Thunder	30.6
Kevin Durant	Warriors	27.6
Kawhi Leonard	Spurs	27.6
Anthony Davis	Pelicans	27.5
James Harden	Rockets	27.4

CHAPTER 5

PASSING FANCY

► Kevin Durant and
LeBron James in action

When the Warriors operate their offense at top speed and efficiency, the ball moves so fast it's hard to keep up. Passes fly from side-to-side, and players dribble rarely. When they do, it's often to set up another pass. The goal is simple: Make the defense move so far, so often, and so quickly that it eventually breaks down. That's usually when a Warriors player is standing alone, ready to hit an open three-pointer. Or one is cutting to the basket for a wide-open layup.

Although many NBA teams prefer to let star players create offensive chances off the dribble, the pass remains the best way to give a defense problems. As mentioned earlier, when Steve Kerr took over the Warriors, he wanted to increase the team's passes per game. He didn't insist his team lead the league in the statistic, but Kerr wanted more unselfish play. He wanted to blend that approach with the kinds of high pick-and-rolls that had helped Steph Curry blossom into a star. In 2016–17, the Warriors finished fourth in the NBA with 318.0 passes per game. The Sixers led the way, with 352.4.

The difference? Golden State had a bunch of great offensive players using the pass to create open shots. Philadelphia was often passing the ball in the hope of getting someone open. It didn't go so well for the 76ers. The team won just 28 games and averaged only 102.4 points per game. On the other hand, Golden State won 67 games, averaged a league best 115.9 PPG, and captured the NBA title.

Passing is important, and so are assists. But as noted earlier, it's important to remember that each team has its own definition of what an assist is. And in some cases, teams want to boost players' individual passing numbers, so assists can sometimes be handed out too generously.

Another way of measuring how successful individuals are at passing the ball is the "secondary assist." In hockey, when a team scores a goal, two players can receive credit for assists. That wasn't the case in the NBA until 2013, when the "secondary assist" or "hockey assist" statistic came into being. Now teams can give credit to the person who makes the pass that leads to the pass that leads to the basket.

Got that?

In other words, if Steph Curry passes up a shot to dish the ball to Kevin Durant, and Durant feeds it to Draymond Green for a layup, Durant gets credit for the assist, and Curry gets the secondary assist.

But not every basket gets a secondary assist, even if there were 10 passes before a field goal. For a player to get a secondary assist, the person who receives his pass must quickly get the ball to the shooter. No more than two seconds and one dribble can take place between that first pass and the one that leads to the score. It can be more difficult to get a secondary assist than to get a regular assist. The rules aren't hard and fast for granting assists. But secondary assists have to fit into a strict set of rules.

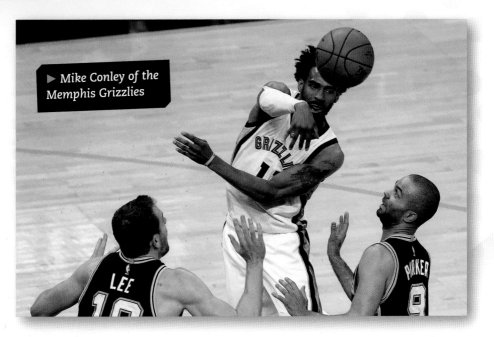

► Mike Conley of the Memphis Grizzlies

In 2016–17, Memphis point guard Mike Conley led the league with 1.3 secondary assists a game. That made sense, since Conley is a pass-first type of point guard. But Isaiah Thomas, then of Boston and the league's third-leading scorer that year, was second (1.2), with Curry (1.1) and Chris Paul (1.0) close behind.

It may not be a statistic that a lot of people talk about, but the secondary assist is helping fans learn more about who the NBA's *real* playmakers are.

Another way to measure a player's ability to make passes count is assist-to-pass percentage. This shows how many of a player's passes result in assists. (The stat is calculated this way: assists divided by total passes thrown.) In 2016–17, Russell Westbrook led the NBA at 18 percent, followed by the Washington Wizards' John Wall (17.7 percent) and James Harden (17.3 percent).

CHAPTER 6

SHOOTING STARS

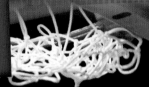

► DeAndre Jordan gets a lot of points on slam dunks—tough shots to miss.

You won't find too many fans who look at the Clippers' DeAndre Jordan and Jazz center Rudy Gobert and consider them offensive powerhouses. In 2016–17, Jordan averaged 12.7 PPG, while Gobert scored 14.0. Both numbers are certainly respectable. But in an NBA where top scorers are putting up 25 to 30 points a night, neither player can be considered a scoring star.

But when it comes to shooting percentages, both are top performers. For years, the NBA measured how well a player shot simply by looking at his overall field goal rate. In 2016–17, Jordan led the NBA by making 71.4 percent of his shots. Gobert was second, at 66.1 percent. That made sense, since both players took the vast majority of their shots close to the basket. Jordan is a lousy free-throw shooter, which shows he isn't a great pure shooter. He makes a lot of short, easy shots. He's not much of a threat away from the hoop.

In the past five years, the NBA has moved beyond the basics of field goal percentage. Now statistics show how well players shoot from all over the court. The league has also combined two-pointers, three-pointers, and free throws to create stats such as true shooting percentage (TSP) and effective field goal percentage (EFP).

TSP covers all kinds of shots. It shows who is best at putting up the basketball from everywhere. A complicated formula considers success from outside the arc, inside the arc, and at the line.

In 2016–17, Gobert led the way with a 68.1 percent TSP. Jordan was second (67.3 percent). It makes sense those two would have high TSPs, since they didn't take many three-pointers (three total), and each shot well from inside the arc. It's surprising that the third-place finisher was Kevin Durant (65.1 percent), who launched 312 three-pointers. It's one thing to be a great overall shooter when your attempts are all from inside 10 feet and from the free throw line. But Durant showed his greatness

▶ Rudy Gobert

by being a threat from all over the court—and by making a very high percentage of all shots.

Effective field goal percentage (EFG) deals only with two- and three-point shots. The idea behind it is that since three-pointers are worth one more point and are shot from farther away than most twos, they deserve extra weight in shooting stats. To calculate effective field goal percentage, add made field goals to the product of 0.5 multiplied by the number of three-pointers made (0.5 x 3P). Then that number is divided by the total number of field goals attempted. So, the final formula is (FG + (0.5 x 3P)/FGA), which adds the two types of field goals—with a multiplier added to give three-pointers more value—divided by all shots taken.

In 2016–17, Jordan and Gobert were at the top of the EFG list, because all but three of their shots were two-pointers. But there were some non-centers close behind. Washington Wizards forward Otto Porter was fifth, thanks to strong three-point shooting (43.4). Durant and LeBron James tied for seventh place, since each can hit the long ball. And Golden State's Steph Curry was 10th. He took 54.7 percent of his shots from behind the arc—and converted 41.1 percent of them. It's remarkable he finished so high on the list. It just shows what a great marksman he is.

Basketball fans have always been drawn to big-time shooters. Thanks to these new statistics, fans are now able to find out who the overall best bombers are and why.

CAREER EFG & TSP LEADERS

Effective Field Goal Rate Career Leaders

	PLAYER	TEAM[S]	EFG
1	DeAndre Jordan	Clippers	67.6%*
2	Tyson Chandler	Bulls/ Hornets/Bobcats/ Mavericks/Knicks/Suns	59.5%*
3	Dwight Howard	Magic/Lakers/Rockets/ Hawks/ Bobcats	58.3%*
4	Amir Johnson	Pistons/Raptors/ Celtics/76ers	58.3%*
5	Shaquille O'Neal	Magic/Lakers/Heat/Suns Cavaliers/Celtics	58.2% (1992–2011)

True Shooting Percentage Career Leaders

	PLAYER	TEAM[S]	TSP
1	DeAndre Jordan	Clippers	68.3%*
2	Cedric Maxwell	Celtics/Clippers/Rockets	63.3% (1977–88)
3	Tyson Chandler	Bulls/Hornets/Bobcats/ Mavericks/Knicks/Suns	62.5%*
4	Artis Gilmore	Colonels/Bulls/Spurs/ Celtics	62.3% (1971–88)
5	Stephen Curry	Warriors	61.9%*

* indicates active player (stats through 2016–17 season)

CHAPTER 7

MINUTE BY MINUTE

▲ Coach Gregg Popovich and veteran guard Tony Parker

When the San Antonio Spurs go on the road, they sometimes disappoint fans of other teams. In recent seasons, fans in other cities have shown up only to see stars on the Spurs bench. Coach Gregg Popovich has never worried one bit about resting his players, even if they aren't injured and even if it costs him a regular-season win. To him, sacrificing victories in February to keep his players fresh for the postseason is worth it. And Popovich doesn't care if people are angry about his tactics.

"I don't think the NBA can do anything about it," Popovich said in March 2017. "At the end of the day, it [stinks] at times where certain guys have to rest, but certain guys need rest. And it's a long, strenuous season, and the NBA does a great job of putting the schedule together as best as they can."

Popovich understands that it is a busy schedule, with back-to-back games, and it's up to the coach to protect his players. He said, "A coach's job is to figure out a way for their team to compete for a championship, not compete for a game."

You won't see Spurs starters playing all 82 games of the season. And if that means six-time All-Star forward LaMarcus Aldridge doesn't play in Los Angeles or Phoenix or Philadelphia, that's too bad for fans in those cities.

That's not the case in Minnesota. Timberwolves coach Tom Thibodeau doesn't believe in resting his players. They don't sit out games. And they don't get a lot of rest during them, either.

In 2016–17, the Wolves bench averaged the fewest minutes (69.7) and points (22.8) per game. Only two players in the NBA played more than 3,000 minutes. Both of them—Andrew Wiggins and Karl-Anthony Towns—played for the Wolves. Only five teams in the league didn't rest a non-injured player in 2016–17, and Minnesota was one of them. Thibodeau is clearly a man who lives for the moment.

But the question is whether his strategy works. In 2016–17, the Timberwolves had a point differential of plus-162 in the first halves of games. That means they outscored opponents by a total of 162 points in the first two quarters. The problem was that they had a minus-253 differential after halftime. Minnesota was great early on, when players were fresh, but as the game continued, the Timberwolves struggled. One reason for that could be that the starters became tired thanks to the long time they spent on the court. The results weren't great. Minnesota finished with a 31-51 record and failed to make the playoffs for the 13th straight season.

During the 2017–18 season, Thibodeau continued to play his starters for big minutes and relied heavily on them for production. The Timberwolves played better than they had, even though a late February injury to star Jimmy Butler forced them to scramble. The Wolves finished with a winning record and made the playoffs.

Like so many other advanced statistics, measuring the minutes the Timberwolves played and their impact provides a deeper look into the NBA and why teams

▶ Jimmy Butler led the Wolves to the playoffs in 2017–18.

win and lose. As time goes on, expect other metrics to emerge. When they do, fans will have the ability to learn more about their favorite players and teams. That will make them more knowledgeable and help them enjoy the NBA even more.

STAT GLOSSARY

assist-to-pass percentage—the number of assists a player earns in relation to the total number of passes he throws; it is calculated by dividing total assists by total passes

assist-to-turnover ratio—found by dividing the total number of assists a player has recorded in a game by the number of turnovers the player has committed in the same game

defensive efficiency—the number of points a team allows opponents to score per 100 possessions.

effective field goal percentage (EFG)—a measure of shooting efficiency that accounts for the fact that a three-point field goal is worth more than a two-pointer

field goal percentage—the ratio of field goals made to the number attempted

offensive efficiency—the number of points a team scores per 100 possessions

pace—the number of possessions a team has during a game or a season or a specific stretch of games

player efficiency rating (PER)—a measure of a player's per-minute productivity; it is calculated by assigning value to all contributions a player can make, both positive and negative

point differential—the difference for a team between the average points its scores, minus the average points its opponents score

points per game (PPG)—the average number of points per game a player or team scores

possessions per game—the average number of times a team has the ball every game

real plus-minus (RPM)—a measure of how a player's team performs while he is on the court compared to how it performs without him; real plus-minus takes into account the strength of the opposition and the performance of the player's own teammates

true shooting percentage (TSP)—a measurement of how well a player shoots from all over the court; two-pointers, three-pointers, and free throws are all part of its calculation

READ MORE

Frederick, Shane. *Basketball's Record Breakers.* North Mankato, Minn.: Capstone Press, 2017.

Omoth, Tyler. *A Superfan's Guide to Pro Basketball Teams.* North Mankato, Minn.: Capstone Press, 2018.

Sports Illustrated for Kids Editors. *Big Book of WHO Basketball: The 101 Stars Every Fan Needs to Know.* New York: Time Inc. Books, 2015.

INTERNET SITES

Use FactHound to find Internet sites related to this book.

Visit **www.facthound.com** Just type in 9781543514476 and go.

Super-cool stuff!

Check out projects, games and lots more at
www.capstonekids.com

INDEX